"Break a Leg!"

A Treasury of Theatre Traditions and Superstitions

by Lisa Bansavage and L.E. McCullough

SILVER SPEAR
PUBLICATIONS

Published by Silver Spear Publications
P.O. Box 352, Woodbridge, New Jersey 07095
United States of America

www.SilverSpearPublications.com

∞~∞~∞

This Edition © 2017 Lisa Bansavage & L.E. McCullough

First Printing: October, 2017

ISBN 978-0-9967889-4-6 (eBook)
ISBN 978-0-9967889-5-3 (softcover)
ISBN 978-0-9967889-6-0 (pdf)

∞~∞~∞

All Rights Reserved. This book may not be transmitted, reproduced or stored in part or in whole by any means without the express written consent of the publisher, except for brief quotations in articles and reviews.

Every effort has been made to acknowledge and obtain permissions for the contents of this book. The publisher will make any necessary changes at subsequent printings.

∞~∞~∞

Front & back cover design by David Simpson Design LLC
www.DavidSimpsonDesignLLC.com

∞~∞~∞

Inquiries: *email us at* SilverSpearPublications@gmail.com
And we will happily respond!

~ CONTENTS ~

~ **FOREWORD** ~

"The theater is a kind of alchemical cauldron of potential magic, for not only does it date back to the earliest times, it is supported by some of the most primitive souls in existence, people one could only compare with the mystical gypsy races of the past, travelling players for whom life is rarely secure and almost invariably dependent on the most powerful gods and fates."

— **Peter Lorie**, *Superstitions* *

EVER SINCE I have worked in the theatre, I have been on a relentless search to find the perfect opening night gift.

On occasion I have been fortunate to find something from the show's theme that speaks to me. Searching through bookstores and gift shops across the country, I have always kept an eye out for a book that relates specifically to the theatre and its myriad of curious traditions and quaint eccentricities.

I never found one and often vowed I would someday write such a book myself.

When I had the good fortune to marry a writer, my dream came true. *"Break a Leg!"* is the result of our treasure hunt to assemble a collection of facts and fancies about the art form that both imitates and transcends reality.

I hope reading it brings you as much joy as it brought us putting it together.

Traditions and superstitions are as vital a part of theatre life as the plays that go up onstage. What goes on behind the curtain is often as fascinating as what happens before the audience.

Read on and enter a world of mystery and magic!

— *Lisa Bansavage*

---

* *Superstitions*, Peter Lorie. New York: Simon & Schuster. 1992, p. 205.

Break a Leg!

IT IS CONSIDERED very bad luck to wish "Good luck!" to an actor (or director or playwright) before a performance. Instead, you should say to him or her, "Break a leg!"

This tradition has been in common use among the theatre community since the early 1900s. At root, it's a vivid expression of irony. Actors worry about the Fates. Fearing over-confidence, no actor will wish another one "Good Luck" before they go onstage. "Break a leg" reverses the luck flow from bad to good, or so runs the circuitous reasoning process.

Eric Partridge, in his *Dictionary of Catchphrases*, suggests that "break a leg" originated as a translation of a similar expression used by German actors: *Hals und Beinbruch* (literally, "a broken neck and a broken leg"). World War I German aviators used the expression before ascending into the skies for battle, and the expression spread to the German stage and then to British and American theater.

꙳ꙭꙫ ꙳ꙭꙫ ꙳ꙭꙫ

Other etymological conjectures:

- To wish another person good luck is to part with it yourself. If you wish good luck to someone else, it could/might/will leave you.

- Ancient Greek audiences used to stamp their feet for approval instead of clapping their hands. Breaking their legs would suggest a highly extreme form of appreciation!

- "Break a leg" is an old military term for "taking a knee", or bending down to one knee and breaking the line of the leg to show gratitude and respect. This derives, perhaps, from the "broken leg bow" common to actors in Elizabethan times. Actors would lower themselves as far as they could go, bending just one knee, while at the same time sliding the other still-straight leg towards the audience, pushing that toe forward along the floor.

  This special bow occurred after several rounds of applause and was a kind of Ultimate Bow. Thus, wishing actors of that day to "break a leg" was a wish for them to perform so wonderfully that the very special broken leg bow would have to be used in thanking the responsive crowd.

- "Break a leg" is a reference to the front curtains. The *leg* is another name for the rope which holds up the main stage curtain. If you have a successful night, the curtains will be raised many times for encores, and in older theatres, they are hand-cranked. Repeated raising and lowering could cause the mechanism to break, thus "breaking a leg".

- After actor and Confederate sympathizer John Wilkes Booth shot and killed Abraham Lincoln in Ford's Theater, he jumped from Lincoln's box to the stage, literally breaking his leg. A huge public outrage was directed against theater folk. Morale was at such a low point for performers, that out of a sense of ironic humor any actor had only to shout "break a leg!" to the other entertainers to spur them on to a good performance.

※ ※ ※

Other frequent benevolent wish-greetings among actors:

- "See you on the green!"
- "Fall down backward!"
- "Give them hell!"
- "Go and perform an impossible action!"
- "Be brilliant!"
- "Enjoy yourself!"
- "Have a marvelous time!"
- "Knock 'em dead!"
- "Toi, Toi, Toi!" (another German expression)
- "Skin off your nose!" — from a time when stage make-up was crude and often resulted in the skin peeling off; the wish implied that actors would be working and therefore having to apply their make-up.

And the classic opening night telegram to Uta Hagen from Dorothy Parker: "A hand on your opening and may your parts grow bigger."

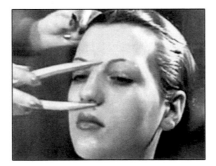

Whistling

DON'T WHISTLE IN the dressing room. Or anywhere in the theatre, especially the backstage area. If you do, things may shake, rattle and roll — very possibly on your head.

Until fairly modern times, scenery was moved about by means of backstage crew members hauling on and letting go of ropes and pulleys. These yeoman workers were often ex-sailors recruited from the navy, their sail-setting and rope-tying skills making them ideal for managing a scenery system that simulated the rigging of a ship.

Among sailors at sea, a shout was the command used to fly the sails out, and a whistle was used to fly them in. Adapted to the theatre, this meant that a scenery change would be cued by a complex whistle code. Any actor whistling backstage could inadvertantly cause a sudden scene change, and all sorts of objects would go whizzing about with frequently dire results.

Whistling in the dressing room might also "whistle up failure" for the show. Or summon the Devil. Or, at the very least, annoy your colleagues by planting an inane tune in their heads.

To undo the harm, the errant whistler must leave the room, turn around three times, knock and re-enter, usually uttering a curse. ✲

Don't Wear Green Onstage

GREEN IS PERHAPS the most shunned color in theatre lore. It is not to be *worn* onstage, it is not to be *placed* onstage, it is not to be involved with the play in any way *whatever*.

Why?

One theory says the belief dates back to when actors performed outdoors on green grass or green stage cloths. Actors wearing green would not be seen well against the verdant fore and backgrounds.

Also in past times, green light was often used to illuminate actors, particularly the villain. This "limelight" would make anyone wearing green appear more or less invisible. *

And everyone knows that green is the Fairies' favorite color, and they are jealous and hostile if mortals don it, even if it is only to impersonate a fairy. ✤

---

* Actually, limelight is white and formed by turning an oxygen-hydrogen flame on a lump of quicklime; but it's a good story!

More Colorful Traditions

FEELINGS IN THE theatre milieu about the *color yellow* are highly jaundiced. It was the color used to denote Satan in the medieval mystery plays, so it has a residual association with evil and death. It is not used in a set or costume unless absolutely necessary.

Certain shades of yellow are also considered unlucky, especially in a tie, vest or hat. In past times, yellow clarinets were forbidden in the orchestra. Yellow roses in a bouquet of flowers are believed to presage the death of an old friend. A yellow dog in the play will bring about a death in the company.

Black is another color often avoided by actors because of its longtime association in Western culture with death. In past times, stage clothing required to appear as black would be made of fabric that was midnight blue but read black under the lights.

The *color blue* has been afflicted at times with a similar negative tinge, it being a belief in past days that wearing blue will cause actors to forget lines. The harmful effect of blue can be cancelled by wearing something silver.

This may derive from the early days of theatre, when blue was a difficult dye color to create and thus very expensive. Any theatre company spending such extravagant amounts on costumes was certain to lose money.

But if the actors were wearing silver, it meant the company was being funded by a benefactor wealthy enough to afford silver adornments.

A related belief among old-time ballet dancers was that any production with blue-painted scenery brought death or loss of salary. Only when the scenery was decorated with silver ornaments would they consent to appear. ✦

✦✦✦

Cats

IT IS LUCKY to have a cat in the theatre, but if one runs onto the stage during a performance — or, worse, crosses the stage — some misfortune will follow. Yet, if the cat makes a mess in the dressing room, this is very good luck!

Needless to say, it is very bad luck to kick or harm a cat in any way. If an actor meets a cat entering the theatre door, good luck is sure to follow. Double good fortune if the feline chooses to brush against the actor while in the theatre!

While the role of the first theatre cats may have been that of Ratter-in-Chief, they soon became prized for their symbolic value as a supernatural force for good.

Several theatres have their "house cats" on "staff" as permanent residents, including such historic venues as the Haymarket Theatre in London and the Théâtre Français in Paris.

London's Adelphi Theatre was home to two cats, a brother and sister called Plug and Socket, who were wont to parade around the stalls. The Aldwych Theatre in London once had a resident jet-black, half-Persian puss who received as much fan mail as many of the actors.

Cats have occasionally taken on acting roles. A cat called Lucky appeared in the play *Watch It, Sailor* at the Aldwych Theatre. A French feline called Mouchi appeared in *The Diary of Anne Frank* at Paris' Montparnasse Theatre. Unfortunately, she suffered from stage fright and occasionally scratched her fellow actors, necessitating frequent claw trims.

A Siamese cat won the part of Pyewacket in *Bell, Book and Candle* at the Connaught Theatre in Worthing, England. His mistress said he would only accept the part if his brother could join him. After some discussion, it was agreed that the supportive brother would wait in the wings as understudy. ✳

Woodcut from the *Thierbuch* (German translation of the *Historiae animalium*) by Conrad Gesner, 1565, Zurich.

Candles & Curtains

THE BASE SUPERSTITION holds that it is unlucky to have candles onstage or in dressing room.

With most theatres crammed to bursting with costumes, fresh paint and make-shift wooden scenery, the origin of this belief is not hard to understand.

More specifically, it is *three candles* that merit objection. One belief is that if three (and only three candles) are lit in a room, the actor closest to the shortest candle will be the first to either marry ... or die. Having three lit candles is also said to provoke quarrels.

❀ ❀ ❀

Curtains for the play? Yes, if an actor looks through the gap in the front curtains to watch the audience entering! Bad luck is sure to follow, at least for that performance.

This superstition has an origin rooted in human psychology. An actor peeking at the audience through the curtain might possibly see something that proves unnerving and disruptive of concentration: friends, family or, worst of all, a stone-faced critic scribbling a review.

❀ ❀ ❀

More curtain lore:

- The looping of a drop curtain is a certain portent of evil (hangman's noose imagery).

- Some actors make a point of touching the curtain when it is finally down.

- It is unlucky to lower the front curtain at the close of a dress rehearsal; this would be regarded by the Fates as a symbol of finality and instigate a bad opening and abbreviated run.

Peacock-a-mamie

THE REPRESENTATION OF the peacock in any form (feathers, fans or peacock designs on the stage or in the audience) is very unlucky.

A possible origin for this belief is that the ever-open *eyes* of the peacock feathers resemble the "Evil Eye" dreaded in folklore around the globe as a portent of terrible misfortune, including death.

The distinguished Shakespearean actress Madame Helena Modjeska (1840-1909) once received an opening night gift of a fan made from peacock feathers.

With a cry of panic, she handed it to her husband, the Count Bozenta, who immediately carried it to the theatre basement and hurled it into the furnace.

When asked why he did not return the gift or pass it on to someone who did not hold that particular superstition, he replied: "The harm would still be there, for Madame had touched it, and therefore it must be destroyed."

In the 1870s, the actor Edwin Booth built a magnificent theatre on Sixth Avenue in New York. He received a large stuffed peacock for an opening gift and placed it prominently in the lobby.

The enterprise failed within two years, bankrupting Booth, who blamed his downfall on "that miserable bird of malignant fate!"

A few years later, another New York City theatre, the Bijou, featured a plethora of painted peacocks all around the auditorium.

The theatre suffered one failed production after another and acquired the reputation of an unlucky venue; the owner finally painted out the peacocks with a coat of bright blue, and overnight, the Bijou became known as one of the luckiest theatres in the business. ❧

Mirror, Begone!

IT IS A LONG-STANDING harbinger of ill luck to use real mirrors onstage. An actor should never look into a mirror over the shoulder of another so that the two reflections are seen together. Doing so will bring certain misfortune to the one overlooked.

The superstition has a basis in reality. Real mirrors on a stage exhibit a tendency to play havoc with a lighting design, reflecting warped rectangles of light into places never intended to be lit, or worse, blinding the actors and audience.

Also, given the much-touted vanity of some actors, a mirror is simply an unneccessary distraction. Polished tin is typically used in place of a mirror; if a real mirror is used, it is smeared with soap to dull the reflection.

This prejudice against mirrors may also date to ancient times when it was believed that if you looked into a mirror, you would see the Devil behind you.

There is a tale of an actor performing in a production of Christopher Marlowe's *Dr. Faustus* that used a real mirror. During the scene where there are six devils onstage, the actor playing Faustus looked in the mirror and saw seven. Assuming it was merely a reflection, he turned and saw that the seventh devil was the Devil himself — El Diablo, Mr. Hobbs, Lou Cypher in the flesh.

The actor died on the spot of a heart attack, and the audience left for home as quickly as they could. No word on whether they received refunds.

Oh, and you probably knew this, but breaking a mirror in the dressing toom is highly unlucky and will result in the standard seven years' bad luck.

Which is pretty much the same as having the Devil in your mirror for seven years, anyhow. ⚜

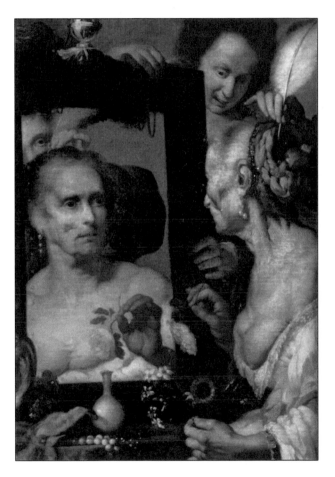

"Vanitas" by Bernardo Strozzi (1630).

Flowers, Jewelry, Thread

TO RECEIVE A bouquet of flowers at the stage door *before* the play begins is an omen of failure.

It is, however, very lucky for an actress to receive flowers *after* a performance.

 Real flowers must never be used onstage. Flowers wilt under strong heat, so if placed on a set, they'll look fairly pathetic after a couple hours under hot lights. There is also an economic imperative — real flowers would have to be replaced each show and would incur ongoing expense.

They also require water (which, if upset during the play, would cause a huge mess). And there is the possibility of allergies causing actors to sneeze (or worse) during a show and certainly providing some unintended comic moments.

In addition to the prohibition against real flowers, other real items are not welcome onstage: real money, real jewelry, real mirrors and real food. Fake items are typically easier to work with and look more "real" from a distance.

Real jewelry reflects the lights in odd and undesired ways. Also, jewelry can often be lost backstage or onstage, giving rise to myriad episodes of distrust and intrigue.

Thread is not to be taken lightly, either.

When an actor finds a thread on another actor, it should be wound around a finger without breaking. This will bring a contract from the management bearing the initial suggested by the number of times the thread goes around the finger; the length of the thread indicates the length of the contract.

Or, if you find a cotton thread on the dressing room floor and wind this around your finger, it's a sign your audition will go well and you will be offered a role. ✦

Bad Dress, Good Show

ACTORS CONSIDER it an ominous sign if a final (dress) rehearsal is perfect. The play will have a very short run, or will go very badly.

Pantomime Rehearsal in "London Theatre-Land" by George R. Sims, 1902.

Similarly, it is extremely unlucky to speak the *tag line*, or the last line of the play, during rehearsals.

The line that completes the play must not be spoken until the opening night of the show, the idea being that a production is never truly complete until it is before an audience.

At times this has caused minor catastrophe when tech crew members who have never heard the final play line in rehearsal either shut off the lights or rang down the curtain early on opening night.

Sunday rehearsals were also formerly considered bad luck. At least, it meant that salaries would not be paid; at worst, that death would occur in the company.

This superstition gained impetus and credence from a bizarre incident involving the Grand Opera House in New York in 1872.

Theatre owner "Jubilee Jim" Fisk had called a Sunday rehearsal of a ballet he had brought over from Europe. The dancers came to the theatre but vehemently refused to rehearse; later in the week Fisk was shot to death in a dispute over one of his mistresses, actress Josie Mansfield, and the theatre world took this as confirmation of the Sunday rehearsal taboo.

Rehearsing the curtain call before the dress rehearsal is also a theatrical faux pas ... the excess hubris tempts the Fates in a mocking way. ❧

A Three-hander Gone Bad: *(l-r) Josie Mansfield, Ned Stokes, Jim Fisk. On January 6, 1872, Stokes shot his romantic rival Fisk to death at a hotel in New York City.*

Opening Night!

ALWAYS A MEMORABLE, excitement-packed and nerve-racked event for any performer, Opening Night in the theatrical milieu has a distinct assemblage of traditions. One of the most unique is the exchange of gifts among cast and crew — perhaps this book is a gift you've given or received!

It's not certain when or where the custom of opening night gifts began, but over the years it has evolved its own etiquette and traditions. Ideally, the gift relates to the show's theme or characters. Some unusual opening night gifts have included:

- Snuff boxes with 18th-century erotic images
  (*Les Liaisons Dangereuses*)

- Gold devil charm (*Damn Yankees*)

- Silver meat pies and silver razors (*Sweeney Todd*)

- Pencils and oranges (*Master Class*)

- Chainsaws (*Fear and Loathing in Las Vegas*)

- Cat food packets (*Cats*)

⁓⁂⁓

Some Opening Night superstitions ...

- If the show is a success on opening night, an actor should not change their costume. If the costume is changed, the show will lose its appeal.

- If an actor receives an opening night telegram, the envelope must immediately be destroyed. Some actors keep one telegram for their next play's opening, as an incitement toward continuity. This goes hand-in-hand with the tradition occasionally encountered whereby an actor always destroys something in the dressing room on the play's last night ... to prevent any evil spirit or residue of failure from following to the next play.

- On opening night, if the first customer pays for a ticket with a torn dollar bill, this is unlucky and the play will close within a week. If the first person in line is an old man, the play will run for a year. (What happens if the first person in line is an elderly gent who wishes to pay with a torn bill? Perhaps the play runs for six months ...)

- For an usher, the first tip of opening night is lucky and must be rubbed against the leg and then kept permanently in the pocket during the run of the play.

- Some producers insist that a woman may not be the first customer on opening night and have been known to discreetly employ a special doorman-lookout for that singular purpose.

- On the opening night of a new play, no person presenting a free ticket shall be admitted until a paid ticket has been deposited in the box — or else the play will net more comps than paid tickets! (And some producers will never give free tickets to a cross-eyed person, *ever*.)

- Some producers open a show on Tuesday, others on an even-numbered day. Some will never open on a Friday or an odd-numbered day. The Shubert Brothers (famous New York producers and theatre owners of the early 1900s) always tried to avoid opening on an "unlucky" Monday.

- Al Jolson never wore new clothes on opening night.

- John, Ethel and Lionel Barrymore gave each other red apples on opening night, which were not to be eaten. This was a tradition inherited from their theatre parents, the legendary Drews. John was also known to drink a jug of apple cider on opening night before and during the performance; once a stage hand drank it by mistake and was fired.

- In the English theatre, to trip on entering the scene on the first night of a play is a sure sign of success. (If an actress trips over the hem of her dress, she should pick it up and kiss it. This will bring a contract in a short time.)

- Before making a first entrance, an actor or actress should be pinched for luck. Maybe this is proof you are not dreaming, nor deceased!

Make-Up

SEVERAL SUPERSTITIONS adhere to make-up and dressing room etiquette, extremely personal subjects for actors throughout the centuries:

- The upsetting of a make-up box is a certain forecast of evil.

- It is unlucky to carry a make-up box or unpack it until after the first night's performance is done — and the reviews in.

- Using make-up with a new set of grease paints on opening night is unlucky.

- Never wear brand new make-up on opening night.

- Make-up boxes should never be cleaned out, as this is said to bring bad luck.

- Powder, if dropped, should be danced upon to bring luck.

- You should use a rabbit's foot to apply make-up.

- If you drop a pair of scissors on the floor, someone else must pick them up.

How Many Actors Does It Take . . .

How many actors does it take to change a light bulb?

All of them. One to do it, and the rest to talk about how much better they could have done it.

How many actors does it take to change a light bulb?

None. Just complain to the director at notes.

How many actors does it take to change a light bulb?

None. Doesn't the stage manager do that?

How many actors does it take to change a light bulb?

Nobody knows. They can never find their light.

How many actors does it take to change a light bulb?

Just one. They hold the light bulb up to the socket and wait while the world revolves around them.

❁ ✾ ❁

10 Things That Bring Good Luck

- Shoes squeaking on your first entrance.

- Precipitation on the day or night of a performance.

- Always exiting the dressing room left foot first.

- Signing a contract under moonlight.

- The stage manager tapping on the stage three times with a stick to drive away the bad spirits.

- The train carrying the company arrives at a station with a cemetery on the right side of the tracks.

- Standing on the edge of the stage and throwing a piece of coal into the gallery (ensures a successful career for a new theatre).

- Spitting into your dancing shoes before putting them on.

- Using a cane onstage.

- Being pricked by a pin at a costume fitting — especially if a bit of blood gets on the costume.

18 Things That Bring Not-So-Good Luck

- Humming inside a theatre.

- Leaving behind a bar of soap in the dressing room; it means you will never play in that theatre again.

- Placing shoes or hats on chairs inside the dressing room.

- Seeing the full moon through glass.

- Putting a hat on a bed or shoes on a table.

- Sharing the stage with children or animals.

- Mentioning the precise number of lines you have in a show (you'll forget some if you do).

- Having a real Bible onstage; it must be an ordinary book painted to look like a Bible.

- The train carrying the company arrives at a station with a cemetery on the left side of the tracks.

- An usher not hearing the first line of the play.

- Wigs.

- Removing a wedding ring to go onstage. If it is truly unavoidable, married actors must cover up the ring with make-up or with masking tape.

- Opening an umbrella onstage … unless you point it to the floor and open downward to indicate all your troubles are "under your feet".

- Using crutches onstage.

- Making the sign of the cross from left to right (it should be made from right to left in the Greek Orthodox manner).

- A woman fainting.

French actress Alice Regnault c. 1880 with parapluie wrongly-pointed.

- Having the following onstage: a real coffin, tin trunks (because they resemble coffins), trunks with cords (because they bring to mind the hangman's noose and the play will be "hanged" with bad reviews).

- Knitting in wings or onstage. Practical reasons: needles are pointy and can rip the costumes of actors rushing by to make an entrance; a knitting needle on the floor may roll under the foot of a stagehand or actor, causing them to fall. Symbolic reason: knitting will "entangle" the production.

ﻋﻠﻴﻚﻋﻠﻴﻚ

Actors on Acting (1)

"People tell me I'm encouraging to young actors. They probably say, 'If that big slob Mitchum can work as an actor, so can I.'"
— *Robert Mitchum*

"I don't become a character. I show a character. I share a character. I share it not only with the audience but with myself." — *Liv Ullmann*

"Modesty in an actor is as fake as passion in a call girl."
— *Jackie Gleason*

"The question actors most often get asked is how they can bear saying the same things over and over again, night after night, but God knows the answer to that is, don't we all anyway? Might as well get paid for it." — *Elaine Dundy*

"I'm an assistant storyteller. It's like being a waiter or a gas-station attendant, but I'm waiting on six million people a week, if I'm lucky."
— *Harrison Ford*

"I never saw an actor lose himself, who did not instantly lose his audience." — *Sir Henry Irving*

"I've always tried to run acting down, tried to be very tough about it, and I don't know why. It's a perfectly reasonable way to make your living. You're not stealing money, and you're entertaining people."
— *Marlon Brando*

"An actor is a sculptor who carves in snow." — *Edwin Booth*

"The real secret of acting is sincerity. Once you learn to fake that, you're in." — *Groucho Marx*

Why Is It Called "the Green Room"?

THE GREEN ROOM is a semi-public lounge where actors can relax and visit with audience members before and after a performance.

The term was in common use by the end of the 1600s, and the *Oxford Companion to the Theatre* entry states that the first published dramatic reference is in Act Four of Thomas Shadwell's play *A True Widow* (1678).

> **Stanmore:** No madam: Selfish, this Evening, in a green Room, behind the Scenes, was before-hand with me.

Some possibilities for the Green Room's etymology:

- Plays originally took place outside on the village green.

- A green-colored room was soothing to actors' eyes after performing in front of harsh lights.

- It was the room where the shrubbery and artificial grass (green carpet) used onstage was stored, making it a cool, comfortable place.

- *Scene, screen* and *green* rhyme. Green Room might actually be a mis-statement of Scene Room where scenery screens were stored.

- The room was walled with green baize cloth as sound proofing, so actors could practice their lines.

- "Green" was stage jargon for the section of the stage visible to the public, so the Green Room was the room nearest the stage.

- It is where the complexion of nervous actors afflicted with pre-show jitters exhibits the tell-tale green hue of nausea.

❋ ❋ ❋

Curiously, the Green Room is rarely painted green these days. Why? Probably because of the theatre superstition that says it's bad luck to paint anything in the theatre green, even the Green Room. ❧

The David Belasco All Star Company relaxing in the Green Room of the Stuyvesant Theatre, New York, 1909. Courtesy: Museum of the City of New York.

The Ghost Light

THE GHOST LIGHT is a single low-watt light bulb or lamp placed onstage and left on when all the other lights in the main house are turned off and the theatre is locked up for the night.

Known also as the "Equity Light" or "Equity Lamp", the ghost light is an obvious aid designed to help the last people going out of the theatre and the first people going in.

Is it also there to keep the resident spooks company overnight?

It's been said that, if all the lights were out, a theatre ghost might think it has been abandoned and wreak mischief on the set.

Other practical and fanciful suggestions for the ghost light's naming and usage:

- To use a simple smattering of sympathetic magic to prevent the theatre from ever "going dark".

- It's a case of confusion with *ghost load* — a tiny, not easily noticeable draw from the power supply (and a specialized lighting term denoting a lantern connected in tandem with a stage practical to ensure the dimmer has enough load on it).

- In the pre-electric era, gaslights acting as pressure relief valves were always kept on, with the resulting flame-flicker giving the appearance of a willow-the-wisp levitating in the darkened house.

- As a holdover from days before theatres were equipped with electric exit lights, the ghost light was maintained to allow firefighters better sight in case they had to suddenly enter the building.

- Once upon a time a burglar broke into a pitch-black theatre and fell off the stage, breaking multiple legs. Though he was clearly trespassing, the crook sued the theatre for maintaining an unsafe workspace. Ever since, theatres took up the custom of leaving a light on to protect themselves from liability. As well as the burglar's ghost ... and that of his attorney.

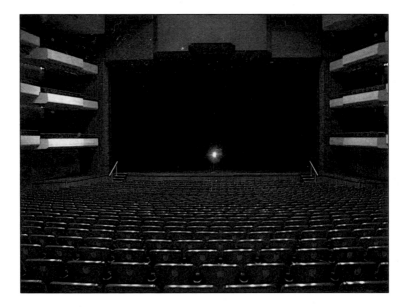

The Gypsy Robe

THE GYPSY ROBE is a "piece" of theatre history that keeps on growing from year to year. It is a wearable trophy that honors the unheralded but vital role in musical theatre played by the chorus dancers and/or singers of a Broadway show — "gypsies" in showbiz parlance.

The tradition began in October, 1950, when chorus dancer Florence Baum, then appearing in *Gentlemen Prefer Blondes* at New York's Ziegfield Theatre, was relaxing backstage in a white satin gown trimmed with marabou. A fellow dancer in the show named Bill Bradley admired the gown and — strictly as a joke — borrowed it to amuse the other gypsies.

The show starred Carol Channing and legendary tap dancer Honi Coles with vocal arrangements by Hugh Martin (composer of *Have Yourself a Merry Little Christmas*) and was a great success. The following week Bradley sent the gown to a friend, Arthur Parrington, due to open in *Call Me Madam* at the Imperial Theatre a few blocks away. Bradley declared this was "the famous Gypsy Robe" and that to wear it backstage and display it to all cast members before opening would bring good luck.

Parrington went along with the gag and staged a mock ceremony. *Call Me Madam* was a success, and the tradition was up and running, with the robe passing next to Forrest Bonshire in the Broadway premiere of *Guys and Dolls*.

Today, just before a Broadway show opens, the cast gathers onstage as the Gypsy Robe is passed to the chorus dancer who has appeared in the most shows. The new recipient nevers knows he or she will be the Chosen One until opening night.

The performer dons the robe and circles the stage three times, as other cast members touch the robe for good luck.

Mementos from each show are sewn onto the robe, marked with show title and date. Along the way, the robe is decorated, painted, patched, stitched and signed by everyone in the show, becoming a fanciful patchwork document of an entire Broadway season.

When all the space on the robe is used up, it is retired to the Museum of the City of New York, and a new robe is started.

Two Gypsy Robes reside in permanent collections at the Smithsonian Institute's National Museum of American History. "Retired" robes are also maintained by Actors' Equity Associtaion at its national headquarters on West 46th Street in New York City, and one is always on display in the Equity Audition Center.

In recent years, the bestowing of Gypsy Robes has been adopted by community theatre and children's theatre groups across the U.S. and Canada. Clearly, it is a tradition with a powerful connection to the core of live drama.

For a list of Broadway's Gypsy Robe recipients from 1982 onward, visit **www.actorsequity.org**. ✤

Following page: Gypsy Robe, 1992-94.
Photo by Carol Rosegg, modeled by Emily Hsu.

How Many Stage Managers Does It Take . . .

How many stage managers does it take to change a—

Done.

How many stage managers does it take to change a light bulb?

I DON'T CARE!!! JUST DO IT!!!

How many stage managers does it take to change a light bulb?

It's on my list ... IT'S ON MY LIST!

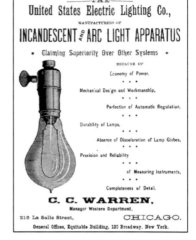

How many stage managers does it take to change a light bulb?

None. Pull the technical director off a set installation to deal with it.

How many technical directors does it take to change a light bulb?

None. Call the master electrician to fix it.

How many master electricians does it take to change a light bulb?

We don't change bulbs, only halogen lamps. It's a props problem.

How many props masters does it take to change a light bulb?

Light bulb?! When did they even *get* a lamp?

How many directors does it take to change a light bulb?

None. Give a note to the stage manager to fix it.

Don't Quote the Scottish Play

ENGLISH PLAYWRIGHT William Shakespeare (1564-1616) wrote 37 plays covering a wide range of human emotion and narrative.

His shortest and most unrelentingly dark play is *Macbeth*, written in 1606 as a specially commissioned piece for England's young King James I (King James VI of Scotland).

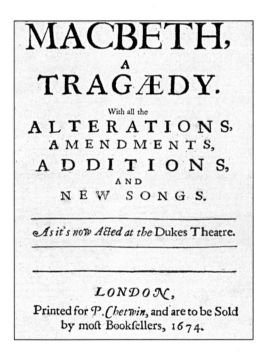

MACBETH,
A
TRAGÆDY.

With all the

ALTERATIONS,
AMENDMENTS,
ADDITIONS,
AND
NEW SONGS.

As it's now Acted at the Dukes Theatre.

LONDON,
Printed for P. Chetwin, and are to be Sold
by most Bookfellers, 1674.

Macbeth is considered the unluckiest play in Western theatre. So unlucky that actors do not even like to mention the title.

They refer to it as "the Scottish Play", "Mr. and Mrs. M", "That Play", "the Plaid Play" or even "the Unmentionable".

An actor will *never* quote any verse from "the Scottish play" before or after a show or in the theatre.

In fact, the sets and props for Macbeth are kept separate from those of other plays, as if possessing psychic contagion.

If you utter this dreaded title by its real name, you must immediately exit the theatre, turn around three times, spit on the ground and then ask for permission to re-enter.

And sometimes break wind, just to be safe.

Or, in some quarters, spin to your left three times, spit over your right shoulder, curse and knock on the door begging for forgiveness ... and possibly be required to quote from *Hamlet*, Act I/Scene 4: "Angels and ministers of grace defend us!"

Whatever. Just do *something*, the spinning and the spitting and the begging being the most important elements of avoiding the torrent of bad luck certain to rain down upon you and the company following your miscue.

Welsh actress Sarah Siddons as Lady Macbeth, 1784.

Why the centuries-old fear and loathing of this well-wrought and compelling dramatization of human depravity and treachery?

At the play's court premiere in 1606, the bad luck began when the boy actor playing Lady Macbeth fell seriously ill with fever just before curtain. Shakespeare himself took his place.

The evening was a disaster, however, performed in a dark hall lit by eerie torches, the actors under-rehearsed and over-worked.

Sitting in the front row was King James, thoroughly appalled by the graphic violence and uncanny parallels with his own personal history and precarious grasp of the throne.

THE
·USA·
FEDERAL [WORK] THEATRE
WPA
PROGRAM

HALLIE FLANAGAN
National Director

PHILIP W. BARBER
Director for N.Y.C.

PRESENTS

THE NEGRO UNIT
in

"MACBETH"

Direct from 12 Weeks Triumphal Run in New York, where 150,000 saw it.

•

"It overwhelms you with its fury and phantom splendor."
—Brooks Atkinson, *New York Times*.

"This Macbeth is the most colorful, certainly the most startling, ever given on this continent."—Burns Mantle, *Daily News*.

"On the opening night of the Negro Theatre production of *Macbeth* Shakespeare himself would have been proud to receive the plaudits of the audience of 'Bravo! Bravo!'"—Ralph Matthews, *Afro-American*.

"I enjoyed the WPA Harlem *Macbeth* more than any other Shakespearian production . . . that I have ever witnessed."—Archer Winston, *New York Post*.

PARK THEATRE
BRIDGEPORT

Evening Performance · · 8:30
Saturday Matinee · · · 2:30

From July 21st to 25th
5 DAYS ONLY

From this opening night fiasco, the play was formally banned in the kingdom until 1611, then performed once at the Globe Theatre, whereupon it disappeared without record until 1667, now massively revised with music, songs, dances and a flying ballet — Macbeth the Musical!

Shakespeare's text was not again presented until 1794. And in the 19th century, very bizarre coincidences of bad luck began plaguing the play worldwide.

✦ ✦ ✦

THE SUPERSTITION derives strength from the play's detailed depiction of witchcraft, a portrayal judged at the time to be so realistic as to flirt dangerously with the Powers of Evil.

Some authorities believe the witches' curses are genuine dark-magic incantations Shakespeare employed to promote a heightened sense of mood, a kind of 17th-century "Sensurround".

It worked ... possibly too well.

Of course, many accidents are liable to occur during *Macbeth* because the play has more than two dozen short scenes with rapid lighting and set changes mostly in dim light or darkness.

Eight scenes require actors in medieval costume to simulate convincing sword fights using axes, daggers, broad swords and other assorted mortiferous weaponry while stumbling around in stage fog or smoke and near-dark. Toss in a few trapdoors, pyrotechnics, odd-shaped battlements, some slippery flooring, and you've got the makings of a real knockabout, slapstick comedy.

Except nobody's laughing.

The play has a history of bringing severe bad luck to its performers, with a staggering number of actors having suffered disaster during or just after productions of the play.

The victim list includes famous actors such as Laurence Olivier, Konstantin Stanislavski, Orson Welles and Charlton Heston, along with scores of lesser-known thespians who have suffered a wide range of accidents, sudden deaths and various psychological traumas.

- In 1703 while *Macbeth* was playing at Covent Garden in London, a freak hurricane struck the English coast, the worst storm in the nation's history. Fifteen hundred people perished, the city of Bristol was destroyed and London itself suffered millions of pounds in damage. Queen Anne declared a day of mourning and theatres closed for a week. This production of *Macbeth* did not re-open.

- On May 10, 1849, fans of actor Edwin Forrest attacked the New York City theatre where English actor William Macready was performing. Troops killed 22 rowdies and wounded scores more in what became known as the Astor Place Riot. The play Macready was performing was *Macbeth*.

- *Macbeth* was Abraham Lincoln's favorite play. He was said to have read it the day before his assassination.

- Legend has it that Lionel Barrymore died while reading *Macbeth* aloud.

With that kind of history, it's no wonder actors believe that by never referring to *Macbeth* by name, they have a chance at warding off the jinx.

And the play's nefarious reach extends to the box office. Theatre managers would often close a weak-drawing play in favor of the crowd-pleasing blood and guts of *Macbeth*. An actor overhearing the play mentioned would immediately fear for his job.

Incidentally, the curse doesn't extend to reading about the play or discussing it outside the theatre ... at least we don't *think* so.

Better turn the page, and be quick about it ... ✤

"Great Riot at the Astor Place Opera House, New York."
N. Currier, 1849. Courtesy: Museum of the City of New York.

St. Genesius and Other Saintly Aids to Actors

ST. GENESIUS IS the patron saint of actors. You don't have to be Roman Catholic or Greek Orthodox to invoke his aid. You just have to need help and believe that some sort of supernatural intervention on your behalf is possible simply by asking for it.

Born in Rome in the late 3rd century C.E., Genesius was a popular comedic actor and playwright.

Legend has it that he converted to Christianity during a play, while performing a baptism scene that mocked the new faith.

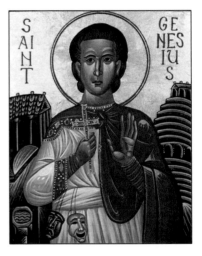

Instead, Genesius startled the audience — which included Roman Emperor Diocletian, a renowned Christian-hater — by delivering an impromptu speech denouncing anyone who persecuted the new religion.

This was a bad career move for Genesius.

Besides being canned from the troupe for his unscheduled improv, he was stretched on a rack, burned with torches and beheaded by personal order of Diocletian.

Talk about suffering for your art.

By the 4th century, Genesius was already being honored as a martyr and was declared a saint in 741 C.E. Genesius' feast day is August 25, and he also serves as patron of comedians, musicians, lawyers, organ makers and secretaries. His intercession can be invoked against freezing and epilepsy — two conditions that not infrequently afflict actors onstage.

It is good luck for an actor to possess a St. Genesius medal. Yet, the actor must receive the medal from someone else; you can't just go out and buy yourself a chunk of divine intercession without somehow earning it on a karmic level.

If you are ever in Rome, Italy, you can visit the chapel of Saint Lawrence located in Santa Susanna's Church. What's left of St. Genesius's mortal remnants is supposedly kept here, and there is a stunning fresco by the Renaissance artist Giovanni Battista Pozzi that depicts Genesius experiencing his onstage conversion.

Directly below the high altar is a memorial to the actor Hugh O'Connor, the son of Carroll and Nancy O'Connor.

≻⋯ ⚚ ≻⋯

The Catholic Church has no shortage of patron saints available for invocation.

St. Vitus, a 4th-century Sicilian martyr and one of the Fourteen Holy Helpers, also serves as a patron saint for actors, along with comedians, dancers, coppersmiths, mummers, sufferers of epilepsy, sleeplessness, snakebite, storms and St. Vitus Dance (Sydenham's chorea, a nervous disorder).

The story of actor Danny Thomas' career success after praying devoutly to **St. Jude**, patron of desperate situations and lost causes, is a well-known part of theatre lore.

Other saintly aids of use to those in creative professions:

- *Musicians/Singers:* Cecilia, Gregory the Great

- *Choir Boys:* Dominic Savio

- *Poets/Writers:* Francis de Sales, David, Columba, Paul, John the Apostle

- *Travellers:* Christopher

- *Difficult Marriages:* Edward the Confessor, Thomas More

- *Television Performers:* Clare

- *Throat Ailments:* Ignatius of Antioch, Blaise

- *Hairstylists:* Martin de Porres

- *Public Relations*: Bernardine of Siena

- *Mental Illness:* Dymphna

- *Diabolical Possession:* Cyriacus

- *Lost Articles:* Anthony

And some saints for the tech crew:

- Hubert (machinists)

- Luke (painters)

- John the Evangelist (paper makers)

- Mark (stained glass workers)

- Francis of Assisi (needle workers)

- Peter (masons)

Followers of non-Western religions may prefer to elicit aid from **Cao Guo-jiu**, one of the Eight Immortals of Daoism and a patron saint of actors in the Far East. He was the brother of a 10th-century Song Dynasty empress and is always shown in court dress holding a pair of castanets. ✦

"You ... you Thespian!"

"THESPIAN" WAS FIRST used as a noun to describe an actor in 1827. But the etymology of the word extends much further back in time.

Tradition holds that a poet named **Thespis** was the inventor of tragedy in the Greek theatre.

Born in early 6th century B.C., Thespis wandered around Athens pulling a handcart, setting up various one-man plays. In 534 B.C. he won the grand prize at the Great Dionysia, a national festival of worship and culture.

Roman Bust of Thespis, 1st-century CE.

Thespis is said to have introduced the idea of an actor speaking separately from the chorus (thus creating "dialogue"), along with other innovations in masks, make-up and costumes.

Thespis, subtitled *The Gods Grown Old*, was the first collaboration of the renowned Gilbert & Sullivan writing-composing team, premiering December 26, 1871, at the Gaiety Theatre in London.

Thespis was received poorly — even the orchestra booed — and it would be three years before the duo worked on another play, *Trial by Jury*, that began their lengthy run of stage success.

Shortly after, the music to *Thespis* went missing and has never to this day been located. Scholars suspect Sullivan burned it. ⚜

Those Happy-Sad Theatre Masks

MASKS HAVE A long and varied history in theatre around the world. The smiling-frowning masks seen in Western theatre symbolizing Comedy and Tragedy derive from the performance tradition of Greek theatre some four or five centuries before the Christian Era.

The faces themselves depict two mythological Greek muses: laughing-face **Thalia** (the muse of Comedy) and crying-face **Melpomene** (the muse of Tragedy).

At that time and place, all actors were male and played multiple roles. An actor donned a mask to show a change in character, gender or mood. In addition, the mask added vocal resonance so that everyone in the huge outdoor ampitheatre could hear.

Members of the chorus also wore masks, usually similar to each other but different from the leading actors.

Each mask had its own shape and color to signify the character or emotion portrayed. Usually the masks were made of linen, wood or leather, and human or animal hair was also used.

A marble or stone face served as a mold. The eyes were fully drawn, but in the place of the pupil was a small hole so the actor could see. The mask mouth was a large opening that permitted speech.

There is no firm date as to when the Thalia-Melpomene mask duo first came to formally symbolize the genre of Theatre. By the 1870s, they were appearing paired-up in programs for various American theatre, vaudeville and minstrel shows, as well as in the occasional commercial advertisement.

By the first decade of the 20th century, the comedy-tragedy masks were seen frequently in theatrical publications from the weekly *Keith's Theatre News* to *The Drama*, a journal published by The Dramatic Publishing Company of Chicago, indicating the symbol as a well-established convention among the theatre community. ✤

Two 2nd-century Roman interpretations
of Thalia (l) and Melpomene (r).

How Many Assistant Directors Does It Take . . .

How many assistant directors does it take to change a light bulb?

One. But he/she has to check with the director first to make sure he/she wants the bulb there.

How many directors does it take to change a light bulb?

Well, um, what do *you* think?

How many lighting techs does it take to change a light bulb?

Nothing happens on that side of the stage anyway!

How many designers does it take to change a light bulb?

www.kliegibros.com

The Players in LIGHT PLOTS

THEY do not dance, nor speak, nor sing; but nevertheless play an important part in every theatrical production. Kliegl spotlights and floodlights are dependable players—never miss their cue, and always do their part well. They enable stage electricians to compose light plots with a nicety of sequence, harmony, and balance, that delights audiences—for more than thirty years of practical experience in show lighting is embodied in their design. Write for an illustrated catalogue of Kliegl stage lighting units. You will find it helpful and inspiring.

KLIEGL BROS

UNIVERSAL ELECTRIC STAGE LIGHTING CO., INC.
ESTABLISHED 1896

THEATRICAL · DECORATIVE · SPECTACULAR

LIGHTING

321 WEST 50th STREET
NEW YORK, N.Y.

Does it have to be a light bulb?

How many theatre students does it take to change a light bulb?

Uh, what's the deadline, 'cause I may need an extension.

How many interns does it take to change a light bulb?

It doesn't matter because you'll have to do it again anyway.

How many lighting designers does it take to change a light bulb?

None. Where's my assistant?

How many electricians does it take to change a light bulb?

Lamp! It's called a LAMP, you moron!

On Broadway

FOR MORE THAN a century, New York City's Broadway has been one of the most vibrant theatre districts in the world.

From the mid-1800s "Broadway" has been synonymous with live commercial theatre in New York, and is today a general term referring to a specific class of big-budget shows playing in nearly 40 theatres clustered within a section of midtown Manhattan bordered by West 41st Street and West 53rd Street and Sixth and Ninth Avenues.

"The Great White Way" is another nickname for Broadway and its theatrical allure, commonly in use since around 1910. Some say it honors theatrical producer George White (1890-1968), who mounted some of the earliest Broadway dance-and-music stage revues.

More likely it derived from a newspaper booster phrase describing the addition of electric street lamps along the street in the 1880s that transformed Broadway into a blaze of illumination and marvel of modern technology. ❄

Producer George White holding auditions for his "George White's Scandals" that ran on Broadway from 1919-1939.

Who the Heck Is Walter Plinge?

"WALTER PLINGE" is the fictitious name traditionally used by English actors to conceal their identity when playing two roles in the same play or to put a name to a role that has not yet been cast at the time the program goes to press.

The tradition began in London theatres during the 1870s, and Walter Plinge's appearance on the bill quickly became regarded as good luck.

According to Wilfrid Granville in the *Theatrical Dictionary*, the original Walter Plinge was a theatre-loving landlord who owned a pub opposite the Theatre Royal, Drury Lane in London and gave unlimited drink and food tabs to the actors. In appreciation, they occasionally allowed him to appear onstage at a benefit in his honor under his own name.

Over the years Walter Plinge has turned up in a wide range of theatrical roles, including two 1933 Laurel and Hardy MGM films (*Me and My Pal* and *The Midnight Patrol*), 1993's U.S. indie flick *Midgets of Atlantis*, a 1930 Australian production of *A School for Scandal* and as the author of two sketches presented in 1997-98 by Polk Street Players in Marietta, Georgia.

Walter Plinge is also the name of a British race horse and the title of the Newsletter of the Imperial College Union Dramatic Society, London. Walter Plinge Day is celebrated on December 2. **Mr. F. Anney** and **Mr. Bart** are other names used for the same purpose in English theatres.

A song from George Spelvin's first stage appearance in "Karl the Peddler".

Plinge's American cousin is named **George Spelvin**, first appearing in 1886 in the Broadway production of *Karl The Peddler* by Charles A. Gardiner and later used even by fairly renowned actors such as Maud Adams and Jacob Adler.

In 1907 the name George Spelvin was used by an actor doing two roles in *Brewster's Millions* by Winchell Smith and Byron Ongley at New York's New Amsterdam Theater. The play was so successful that the authors continued to use the name in the rest of their productions for luck.

Political satirist Westbrook Pegler used Spelvin as an Everyman-type mouthpiece for social comment in his 1942 book *George Spelvin, American, and Fireside Chats*. Depending upon the nationality of the character, he has also appeared as Gregor Spelvanovich, Georges Spelvinet, Giorgio Spelvino and George Spelvinsky.

November 15 is oft-cited as George Spelvin's Birthday, and he was the subject of an anonymously-penned play titled *Who Killed George Spelvin?* that ran during the 1954-55 and 1981-82 seasons at the Albany (New York) Civic Theater.

A one-act by Christopher Durang, *The Actor's Nightmare*, also dramatized the Spelvin legend, premiering at Playwrights Horizons in 1981.

Harry Selby is sometimes substituted for George Spelvin; to date Harry has appeared in nine Broadway shows, including *Button, Button* (1929), *Juno and the Paycock* (1940) and *Anne of a Thousand Days* (1948).

58

In 1966 *Playbill* editor Leo Lerman began a series of annual Spelvin Luncheons publicizing new shows opening on Broadway; the tradition was recently revived by the Spelvin Society of New York.

And, yes, George has a sister. **Georgina Spelvin** was used by Broadway actress/dancer Dorothy May to disguise her portrayal of Miss Justine Jones in the 1972 adult film *Devil In Miss Jones*. ❦

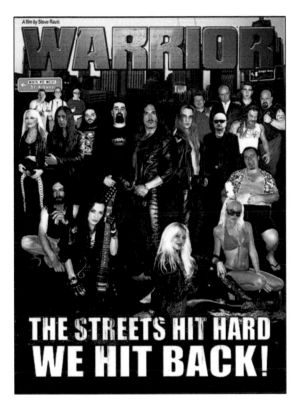

Walter Plinge and George Spelvin
both appear in the 2011 Australian
music film "Warrior".

The Number 13

SOME SUPERSTITIOUS FUN with *triskaidekaphobia* (fear of the number 13):

- If there are 13 in the company at the start of a show, three will get fired before it ends.

- In many American theatres, it is considered good luck to begin the show 13 minutes late — perhaps arising from the notorious lateness of American audiences.

- Many theatre managers will not open a show on Friday the 13th.

- Usher superstition: if the first person in the audience sits in Row M (13th row), it will be a bad night with a lot of chaos. If a patron actually sits in the 13th seat of Row M, they must be carefully watched for signs of trouble: rowdiness, illness, accident, etc.

- Dudley Moore once wrote: "I'm not really superstitious, but if my play opened on Friday the 13th, and I found myself in dressing room 13 on the 13th floor, and the theatre street address was Number 13, then I might think that things were beginning to stack up on me."

- In *Romeo and Juliet*, Juliet is 13 years old, is the 13th named character to enter the play and her full name (Juliet Capulet) has 13 letters — as does "Romeo Montague" ... based on the dates supplied in the lengthy dialogue between the Nurse and Lady Capulet in Act I, Scene 3, the play ends 13 days before Juliet's 14th birthday.

- In *The Producers*, chronic failure Max Bialystock is described as "the biggest name on Broadway — 13 letters."

- Eddie Cantor would rewrite the entire script if his copy was 13 pages long.

- Noel Coward reported that he followed only one superstition: never to sleep 13 people in a bed.

Not the first, nor last member of the acting profession to seek political office.

Some Unusual Theatre Terms

OVER THE CENTURIES, theatre has developed its own occupational vernacular, its own linguistically unique way of ordering the universe with colorful terms and phrases.

- **Aside.** Lines spoken by an actor to the audience and not supposed to be overheard by other characters onstage.

- **Barn Door.** A device fitted into the gel frame holder of a lighting instrument consisting of four pieces, used to direct or focus the light beam.

- **Bastard Prompt.** The position of the prompt desk (usually placed stage left) when placed stage right.

- **Belt Voice.** A musical theatre term denoting a singing voice that can "belt out" songs; as opposed to a *Legit Voice*, suited for classically-oriented material.

- **Black Hole.** An accidentally unlit portion of the stage.

- **Book Flat.** A two-fold piece of scenery that is free-standing when angled open to allow quick setting and compact storage.

- **Bo'sun's Chair.** A small seat or cradle rigged on a rope over a pulley whereby a technician may be hoisted to work at an otherwise inaccessible position.

- **Catwalk.** A narrow walkway suspended between "fly floors", the raised areas from which scenery and drops are flown.

- **Chewing the Scenery.** An actor who gives a completely hammy and over-the-top performance is said to be "chewing the scenery".

- **Corpse.** To break up laughing while playing a scene.

- **Dressing the House.** To seat the audience in such a way as to make it appear larger than it is.

- **Flemish Eye.** Stage hand term denoting a quick eyesplice in six-strand wire ropes.

- **Fuller's Earth.** Any variety of clay that can decolorize oil or other liquids without chemical treatment. Also known as "bleaching clay", fuller's earth is used for make-up, props, wardobe and set dressing needs.

- **Gobo.** A thin metal plate etched to produce a design (foliage, city scapes, windows, etc.) which is projected by a profile spotlight. Possible origins for the word include: an acronym for Graphical Optical BlackOut; short-hand for Go-Between, since the gobo goes between lens and amp; slang for "GO BlackOut", a director's order to eliminate extraneous light from the stage.

- **Going Dry.** Term for an actor forgetting their lines during performance. (*synonyms:* to airplane, ascend, balloon, blow up, chase a kite, fluff, stick)

- **Grand Guignol.** Originally from Le Grand Guignol theatre in Paris, this is a late 19th-century genre of shock theatre specializing in the macabre and gruesome to the delight and horror of the audience.

- **Heads on Stage.** A shouted warning for staff to be aware of activity above them (often just "Heads!"); also used when an object is being dropped from above.

- **Marie Tempest Hinge.** A door hinge reinforced by a screw lever to keep the door from opening by itself on a raked stage; named after the English actress (née Mary Susan Etherington) who lived from 1864-1942.

- **Piano Dress.** A technical rehearsal with actors in costume but using a piano as a substitute for the orchestra, allowing the director to concentrate on technical problems rather than musical ones.

- **Rain Box.** A box or tray containing pebbles or dried peas used to produce a sound effect approximating rain.

- **Raked Stage.** A sloping stage raised at the upstage end.

- **Thinking Part.** A role that includes no spoken lines; more commonly found today in television and films.

- **Thunder Run.** The long channel down which a cannonball is rolled to give a realistic thunder rumble effect. This was formerly built into the roof of older theatres, but mostly now is unused (for safety reasons).

- **Tormentor.** The curtain or flat on each side of the proscenium opening used to regulate the width of the opening.

- **Trap.** This is an opening through the stage floor and includes various sub-categories including *grave trap*, *cauldron trap*, *star trap*, *bristle trap*, *Corsican Trap* and the *Vampire Trap* invented for James Planché's 1820 adaption of Polidori's *The Vampyr*. The Vampire Trap consisted of two spring leaves that parted under pressure and immediately reclosed. Placed in the floor or stage wall, it could give the impression a figure was passing through solid matter.

- **Vomitory.** An auditorium entrance or exit going up through banked seating from below; an architectural feature of coliseums dating from Roman times.

Dame Marie Tempest, DBE.

Grand Guignol poster.

How Many Playwrights Does It Take . . .

How many playwrights does it take to change a light bulb?

Change? Why does it have to change? No changes, it's perfect just the way it is!

How many audience members does it take to change a light bulb?

Three. One to do it, one child to cry and one to say loudly, "ROSE, HE'S CHANGING THE LIGHT BULB."

How many theatre critics does it take to change a light bulb?

All of them. <u>One</u> to be highly critical of the bulb's design elements, <u>one</u> to express contempt for the glow of the bulb, <u>one</u> to observe how trite the use of a lightbulb was, <u>one</u> to lambaste the interpretation of wattage used, <u>one</u> to critique the performance of the bulb itself, <u>one</u> to recall superb light bulbs of past seasons and lament how this bulb fails to measure up, and <u>all</u> to join in the refrain reflecting on how they could build and direct a better light bulb in their sleep.

How many producers does it take to change a light bulb?

None. Why do we need another light bulb?

Famous Actors and Their Superstitions

FOR MANY ACTORS, good luck is maintained by a mascot or charm, a talisman of sorts carried in a costume onstage or kept in the dressing room.

Some famous actors have handed down their stage props (canes, watches, rings) to a younger actor they believe one day might succeed them in their craft.

Continuity is crucial. An actor may keep a prop from their previous play — if the play was a good experience, naturally!

- **Monique van Dooren** kept a lucky black dress near at hand during a show ... **Cecil B. de Mille** wore riding breeches for luck ... **John Ford** liked to direct films in his "lucky" hat ... **Van Johnson** had a pair of lucky red socks and always wore them in his films ... **Ed Wynn** always wore the same pair of shoes when performing; he made one pair last 20 years ... **Kitty Carlisle Hart** always wore a tweed suit for film tests, even in the heat of the summer.

- **Bette Davis** had a gold beetle charm and occasionally delayed the curtain if it could not be found at showtime; she also kept a box of theatre programs from her early days at Cape Cod Playhouse in her dressing room ... **Joan Crawford**, Davis' frequent arch-rival, kept in her dressing room a red belt she had worn in *The Guardsman*, a successful play early in her career.

- **Greta Garbo** had a rope of real pearls that never left her person ... **Fanny Brice** wore a Chinese lucky ring ... **Carole Lombard** carried a smooth round pebble for luck, a gift from husband Clark Gable ... **Pat O'Brien** favored four-leaf clovers, **George Brent** was partial to an Irish shilling ... **Gregory Peck** held on to a script holder he received from **David O. Selznick** from his appearance in *Duel in the Sun* ... **Humphrey Bogart's** talismans included a silver cocktail shaker, a gold Egyptian scarab and five German army helmets.

⌒) (⌒

MANY ACTORS INDULGE in a wide range of behavior-based superstitions, typically obsessive-compulsive and always highly personalized:

- **Dorothy Lamour** would never pick up an umbrella if she dropped it; if no one was there to pick it up, she would leave it ... **Spencer Tracy** considered it bad luck to go back and collect a forgotten object ... **Tyrone Power** thought it bad luck to eat baked potatoes on Friday ... **Lynn Fontanne** and **Alfred Lunt** would never cross anybody on a staircase ... **Jack Lemmon** always whispered the words "magic time" before entering a scene.

- After his success in *Frankenstein*, **Boris Karloff** always used the same dressing room, the same hallway to get there and always entered the studio by the same gate; he insisted on having the same dresser, same make-up man and the same table in the studio cafeteria throughout his career at Universal.

- **Jack Pearl** always touched his ear for good luck before starting a show; if anyone else did it, he would have to touch the other person's ear before going onstage. Once a practical joker touched Pearl's ear on a Broadway opening night and ran off minutes before curtain; Pearl went wild and followed the man out of the theatre all through midtown Manhattan before catching up to him and tweaking his ear.

- **Tallulah Bankhead** had several superstitions. "You name it, honey, I believe in it," she affirmed. Champagne was lucky and was drunk in quantity before, during and after a show. Visitors to her dressing room had to enter with their right foot first, the left foot deemed unlucky; if someone entered incorrectly, they were ordered out and made to re-enter right foot first. Ms. Bankhead's favorite mascot was a hare's foot given to her by her father; she carried the foot everywhere and was buried with it.

✺)(✺

CERTAIN ACTORS are considered good luck in themselves and are believed to guarantee the success of a play or film by their mere presence — **Vivien Leigh**, **Gladys Cooper** and **Mrs. Patrick Campbell** were among this select group.

John Wayne considered **Ward Bond** his personal good luck charm and made sure he was in all his pictures until Bond's career as a leading TV actor took off. The "Six Degrees of Kevin Bacon" game retains elements of this belief in its linking of disparate actors.

Other actors are considered bad luck for various reasons. The story is told of an actor in London who, after accepting a role in a play, asked about the other cast members. As their names were recited, he grew increasingly unnerved and finally shouted, "That's not a cast list! It's a suicide pact!" ✦

Edmund Kean's Most Peculiar Charm

THE GREAT ENGLISH actor **Edmund Kean** (1787-1833) spared no effort when searching for a suitable lucky charm.

On a visit to America in 1820, he caused the remains of another great English actor, **George Frederick Cooke** (1756-1812), to be re-buried in another spot in St. Paul's Churchyard in lower Manhattan.

Edmund Kean as **Hamlet**.

Kean had the casket opened and appropriated one of Cooke's toe bones (some authorities claim it was a part of the forefinger), which he preserved for many years as a favorite talisman.

When Kean returned to England, the company from the Drury Lane Theatre were on hand to meet him.

"Before you say a word, my friends, behold!" he declared, proudly displaying his relic.

"This is the toe bone of the greatest creature that ever walked the earth — George Frederick Cooke. Come, down with you all, and kiss the bone!"

Each actor in his turn fell upon his knees and kissed the shriveled black appendage with great ceremony.

Kean preserved the relic for many years, until one day his wife flung it out the window, probably in a fit of anger over Kean's frequent alleged extra-marital socializing. Kean never knew what became of his talisman, and in mourning its loss would frequently say to his fellow actors: "I feel as if I had lost my dearest friend."

Another tale holds that Cooke's skull, which was not buried with him, appeared onstage some years later ... in the role of Yorick during a production of *Hamlet* starring **Edwin Booth**. ⚜

George Frederick Cooke as
Gloucester in **Richard III**.

Stage Turkeys and the Notorious Broadway Moose

BEHOLD THE STATELY turkey and the noble moose — two unassuming denizens of the animal kingdom that have become stigmatized among theatre lovers as synonymous with utter, complete and total failure, as in "What a turkey!" or "That play is a moose!".

"Turkey" has been a showbiz slang term for an inferior show or flop since the 1920s and was probably derived from the image of the turkey as a stupid bird.

Another possibility is that, in the early 1900s, anywhere from 100 to 250 shows ran on Broadway a year. A large number of them opened during the Thanksgiving-Christmas season due to the producers' belief that customers would attend any show at all, whatever its merits, simply because it was offered as holiday fare.

Thus, even a bad show was virtually guaranteed a profit if it opened during "turkey time".

Richard Hugget in his book *Superstition on Stage* mentions another source, possibly apocryphal: a turn-of-the-20th-century Broadway play titled *Cage Me a Turkey* that closed before the end of its opening performance.

At intermission a fight erupted between company members, and several were hospitalized; the second act was never presented. Among the set decorations were a stuffed turkey and a stuffed peacock.

✦ ❀ ✦

Moose Murders by Arthur Bicknell opened and closed the same day, February 22, 1983, at the Eugene O'Neill Theatre in New York.

While there had been other Broadway shows that lasted only a day (or closed before opening while still in previews), the flagrantly nonsensical nature of *Moose Murders* (sub-titled "A Mystery Farce in Two Acts") earned it immediate and lasting notoriety as a shining standard for theatrical non-excellence. It has been immortalized on the Wall of Flops at Joe Allen's eatery in Manhattan.

Though *Moose Murders* failed on Broadway, it still occasionally turns up at high schools, colleges and community theatres, indicating that, like cats, moose have more than one theatrical life. ✻

"Broadway Moose", a sketch by Don Nute.

Theatre Ghosts

THEATRES ARE PROUD of having a resident ghost. In fact, it seems no self-respecting theatre manager with a claim to upholding time-honored thespic tradition would admit they *don't* harbor some supernatural hanky-panky within their walls.

The oldest theatre ghosts, naturally, inhabit British Isles theatres. At the **Theatre Royal, Margate**, there is a "laughing ghost" who chuckles at lines spoken onstage and also delights in playing havoc with the lights. This is believed to be Sarah Thorne, a former theatre manager from the mid-1800s.

John Buckstone (1802-1879). Actor, playwright, ghost.

The ghost of the **Haymarket Theatre Royal, London**, is seldom seen but often heard, opening and closing doors, walking through the halls and casting a strong though invisible presence felt by many actors in their dressing rooms.

It is thought to be John Buckstone, manager of the theatre from 1853-78. Buckstone was known to be Queen Victoria's favorite theatre manager and often sat with the Queen in her royal box.

❃ ❃ ❃

Eden Court Theatre, Inverness, Scotland, is built upon the site of a bishop's residence. Theatre patrons have seen a Green Lady appear, said to be the wife of a bishop who hung herself in the chapel, along with a small girl and a priest said to have murdered his family — nearly as much drama occurring offstage as on.

The **Palace Theatre, London**, is haunted by the ghost of Welsh-born actor and playwright Ivor Novello (1893-1951), who died during a run of his last musical, *King's Rhapsody*. Novello's ghost is said to watch performances from the back of the dress circle.

Ivor Novello in "The Lodger: A Story of the London Fog", 1927.

Two decades later an actress auditioning for *Jesus Christ Superstar* prayed to him before she went onstage; she got the part ... and Novello's former dressing room.

The ghost of another prominent Welsh literary figure, Dylan Thomas, has been glimpsed in the **Bush Theatre, London**, quietly observing the proceedings.

⊱━❀❋❀━⊰

A FEW GHOSTS ARE distinctly time-sensitive. "The Man in Grey", a resident ghost of **Theatre Royal, Drury Lane, London**, is a daytime ghost who apparently favors matinees and appears only in the morning and afternoon at rehearsals. Dressed in the early 1800s attire of an urban gentleman, he is often taken for one of the actors or a costumed usher and has been seen by hundreds of performers and audience members over the years. If the Man in Grey appears during rehearsal or performance, it is a good omen for the show's success.

His counterpart in color is "The Grey Lady" of **Theatre Royal, Bath**, a young woman dressed in 18th-century evening attire with feathers in her hair and frequently seen sitting at several points throughout the theatre. She may have killed herself over an unfortunate affair with an actor. Another off-the-books Theatre Royal employee is a Phantom Doorman, likewise dressed in 18th-century clothes, who has been spotted only by cast members.

A ghost named Rose is sometimes seen sitting in the stalls before a performance at the **Royal Shakespeare Theatre, Stratford**. Visitors see a woman in their seat and request her to move — only to be asked by the usher why they are talking to thin air!

Several Liverpool theatres (**The Empire, The Epstein, Liverpool Playhouse**) are enlivened by a cast of spectrals that include a ghostly schoolboy, a tall man with his head crooked sideways, a thin woman from the 1930s and "Old Pasty Face", a dour-looking gentleman whose appearance during a production presages the show will soon close.

The Epstein Theatre, formerly known as the Neptune, was renamed in 2011 after Beatles' manager Brian Epstein. To date, there have been no paranormal sightings, or soundings, of any musical celebrities. But, then again, "Tomorrow Never Knows".

❀ ❀ ❀

SOME GHOSTS ARE helpful and aid actors in putting on outfits and getting onstage.

The **St. James' Theatre, King Street, London**, now demolished, had a dressing room ghost who provided the added service of brushing down actors before their entrance.

Famed 19th-century actor Joseph Grimaldi established himself as the greatest of English clowns at **Sadlers Wells Theatre, London**, where a white-painted face has been repeatedly glimpsed sitting in the boxes.

Grimaldi apparently splits his ethereal workload at Theatre Royal, Drury Lane, helping actors with costumes and steering them to good spots onstage.

The Theatre Royal has another ghost believed to have been an actor or even director. On occasion this ghost has not been so benevolent; an early 20th-century actor in the midst of a soliloquy from *Falstaff* once felt a sharp kick in the backside.

Hearing of the incident, producer Sir Henry Irving declared, "That settles it. The ghost isn't an actor, he's a critic!"

⊱⋅⋆⋅⊰

William and Jessie – still together in the Afterlife?

Actresses in dressing rooms at **Adelphi Theatre in the Strand, London**, occasionally hear two quick taps on their dressing-room mirror — a courtesy call from William Terriss, the popular actor/manager stabbed to death in 1897 outside the Adelphi stage door by a severely disgruntled fellow thespian.

Terris died in the arms of his leading lady, Jessie Millward, and his last words were, "I will come back". Over the last century, he has appeared to fulfill his parting promise on numerous occasions.

But for sheer long-lasting occult hostility, it's hard to match the phantom-filled jacket hanging around the **Duke of York's Theatre, London** since the eaarly 1900s.

A bolero jacket has been strangling the actors who wear it, causing feelings of panic and fear of something terrible about to occur. Though comfortable at the original fitting, every time it was worn, it became tighter and even suffocating.

After one actress wore it, red marks covered her throat, as if someone had been strangling her. A séance was promptly held that revealed the jacket had originally been worn by an actress strangled to death in the theatre by a jealous boyfriend.

❀ ❀ ❀

THEATRE GHOSTS FLOURISH on either side of the Equator down to the very Antipodes.

In Australia, you'll find Elizabeth the Teenage Ghost livening up the proceedings at Brisbane's **Twelfth Night Theatre**, nine dancing ghosts at Elsternwick's **Classic Cinema** (formerly a dance hall), and the ghost of opera singer Federici (*aka* Frederick Baker) at Melbourne's **Princess Theatre** — he died there in 1888 of a heart attack while falling through a trapdoor during Gounod's *Faust*.

And though they haven't been around as long as their Old World counterparts, American theatres possess a wide-ranging selection of spectral spectators.

- **Van Meter Hall, Western Kentucky University, Bowling Green, Kentucky.** The ghost is a stage hand who fell onto the stage in 1910; during performances a red light shines on the spot where the man fell.

- **Kimo Theatre, Albuquerque, New Mexico.** On opening night actors leave a donut for the ghost of a six-year old boy who died in an accident there in the 1950s.

- **Le Petit Theatre du Vieux Carre, New Orleans, Louisiana.** The house haunt is Miss Caroline, an actress in a wedding dress who toppled to her death from the roof of this French Quarter theatre in the 1800s; she appears on the back stairway and oftens help find missing objects.

- **Ford's Theatre, Washington, D.C.** On April 14, 1865, President Abraham Lincoln was shot and killed by actor John Wilkes Booth. Many actors claim to have felt an occult presence in the theatre, which reopened in 1968 after being closed for decades. There are footsteps in an empty theatre, lights going on and off, curtains rising and lowering without human hands, strange voices laughing and crying. The stage even has an invisible "spirit line" marking the ziz-zag path Booth took while escaping. Actors standing on or near the line are seized with strange feelings; they forget lines and cues, tremble and feel nauseous. Esteemed actors Hal Holbrook and Jack Aronson have reported they felt a noticeable drop in temperature as they crossed this line of evil.

- **Blair Hall Theatre, Sinclair Community College, Dayton, Ohio.** A spirit couple dances back and forth on stage, and actors claim to feel invisible tuggings. Of course, the theatre is built on the site of a former public gallows.

- **Barter Theatre, Abingdon, Virginia.** Ghosts dating from before the Civil War prowl the stage and dressing rooms of this former stop on the Underground Railroad.

- **Belasco Theatre, New York City**. This theatre is responsibly and regularly haunted by the lively spirit of its namesake creator, actor/impresario David Belasco (1854-1931), renowned during his colorful lifetime for wearing a monk's habit and decorating his room in the style of a monastery. The ghost has been glimpsed sitting in Belasco's favorite stage box, and sounds of an elevator moving up and down can be heard when the theatre is empty — though the elevator was disconnected long ago.

- **Palace Theatre, New York City.** A shadowy tightrope walker has been seen swinging away from the dress-circle rim and then falling with a piercing scream. This is believed to be the ghost of Louis Bossalina (AKA Borsalino), a vaudeville acrobat who fell during a show at the Palace in 1935. It is not considered a good omen if you see the ghost or hear the scream.

⁕⁕⁕

THEN THERE IS the **Fulton Opera House, Lancaster, Pennsylvania**, the oldest theatre in continuous operation in the U.S. and a facility that may own the distinction of America's Most Haunted Theatre.

According to playwright Barry Kornhauser, the theatre's education director and historian, the Fulton was built in 1852 on ground far from hallowed — the site of a pre-Revolutionary War county jail and a terrible massacre in 1763 of local Native Americans by colonial vigilantes.

Marie Cahill.

Which may explain the oft-registered instances over the years of doors mysteriously opening and closing, figures in 1700s Indian dress sporting along the aisles, a white mist floating about the orchestra pit and several spirit presences including that of the French actress Sarah Bernhardt (who performed at the Fulton in 1912), actor John Durang (one of the first American-born actors of the 18th century and a Lancaster native) and actress Marie Cahill (1866-1933), the theatre's own ghostly Woman in White.

One of the Fulton's more spectacular and public paranormal episodes occurred in the mid-1990s when pianist/actress Pamela Ross was performing her *Carreño* show in front of an audience of 300 patrons.

During Ross' rendition of Lizst's *Mephisto Waltz*, the piano erupted in sudden protest: three strings snapped, two hammers broke, a key flew off the keyboard into the air as three stage lights exploded overhead, raining showers of metal and glass upon the stage and a very surprised Ross.

Was this one of the resident Fulton ghosts objecting to the choice of material?

Or possibly the indomitable spirit of 19th-century Venezuelan pianist Teresa Carreño (1853-1917), the subject of the show, throwing a prima donna fit? ✤

Teresa Carreño.

Actors on Acting (2)

"Acting is a form of confession." — *Tallulah Bankhead*

"Remember: there are no small parts, only small actors."
  — *Konstantin Stanislavski*

"I love acting. It is so much more real than life." — *Oscar Wilde*

"I was a good, small-town girl. Acting gave me the opportunity to do outrageous things. It allowed me to be sad, happy, angry and lustful, even if it was just vicariously." — *Joan Allen*

"To be a good actor, it is necessary to have a finely tempered soul, to be surprised at nothing, to resume each minute the laborious task that has barely just been finished." — *Sarah Bernhardt*

"I am in the mood to be all kinds of women on the stage."
  — *Dame Judith Anderson*

"He is blessed who can escape from the absurd artificiality of living into the reality of theatre." — *Theodore Bikel*

"You spend all your life trying to do something they put people in asylums for." — *Jane Fonda*

"There used to be a real me, but I had it surgically removed."
  — *Peter Sellers*

✤ ✤ ✤

Clackers

THE "CLAQUE" IS a unique element of theatre history. From the French word *claquer*, "to clap hands", the claque is an organized body of professional applauders — *claqueurs* or, in modern parlance, *clackers* — hired by theatre managers to arouse and guide positive audience response.

The idea goes back to ancient times. Legend says that when the Roman emperor **Nero** acted in palace theatricals, he made certain of favorable reviews by having five thousand Roman soldiers on hand to chant cheery slogans praising his performance.

A 16th-century French playwright, **Jean Daurat**, revived this idea and bought up blocks of tickets for his plays, giving them free to whoever promised to voceriferously express their approbation.

The 19th century was the heyday of claqueurs. In 1820 an enterprising Parisian, **Monsieur Sauton**, opened a *claqueur* supply office from which the manager of a theatre would order a desired number of *claqueurs*.

A *chef de claque*, a sort of foreman, would distribute the *claqueurs* at strategic points in the theatre and decide when applause was needed, what form it would take and for what length.

Claqueurs were divided into sub-groups: *commissaires*, who knew the show by heart and called the attention of their neighbors to its dramatic points; *rieurs*, who laughed loudly at the comedy; *pleureurs*, generally women, who faked crying and other tearful outbursts; *chatouilleurs*, who kept the audience in a good humor with jokes; *bisseurs*, who clapped their hands and shouted *Bis! Bis!* to secure encores.

By 1830 the claque had become an established institution in European theatre, a fact of performing life that was feared yet accommodated. Without support of the claque, new performers had little chance of breaking out of obscurity and achieving stardom.

These days, public etiquette dictates that theatre audiences remain mostly silent and not interrupt the performance with orchestrated applause or antics — except for *The Rocky Horror Picture Show*, of course. ✤

Depiction of Paris theatre claquers, 1864,
by Honoré Daumier.

Odds & Ends

IF AN ACTOR replaces another during a long run, it is bad luck and bad manners for the incoming actor to see the outgoing actor's final performance. It's equally bad luck for the outgoing actor to see the incoming actor's first show, nor should a good-luck telegram be sent.

❧

RENOWNED ABOLITIONIST author Harriet Beecher Stowe believed theatre was immoral and at first refused to allow her popular novel *Uncle Tom's Cabin* to be adapted to the stage. When she finally did attend a performance of her work, she came hidden under a shawl.

❧

ENGLISH THESPIAN Edmund Kean frequently performed with local stock companies, arriving the day of the show and then going to his lodgings to rest until curtain. On one occasion, the company manager asked Kean what time he wanted the actors to meet for rehearsal.

"Rehearse?" replied Kean. "I'm not going to rehearse. I'm going to sleep."

"But, sir," persisted the manager. "The company … have you any instructions for them?"

"Instructions!" roared Kean. "Tell them to keep a long arm's length away from me and do their damned worst!"

❧

WORLD'S SHORTEST PLAY: *Anu* (24.13 seconds) by S.L.N. Swamy premiered Aug. 15, 1999, in Bangalore, India, eclipsing the record of 30 seconds held since 1969 by Samuel Beckett's *Breath*. *Anu* features 24 actors and dialogue consisting of "nataka, nataka, na ... Taka" (drama, drama, drama).

WORLD'S LONGEST PLAY: *Sarathya*, also by S.L.N. Swamy, runs 51 hours and premiered Aug. 15-17, 1999, also in Bangalore. It features 200 songs and links the ancient Indian epic *Mahabharata* to present-day politics.

Source: Guinness Book of World Records

⁂

SARAH BERNHARDT'S recipe for a successful acting career and eternal youth: "Eat lemons, work hard and say your prayers to the dear God."

Sarah Bernhardt, 1891, in the role of Cleopatra.

DEFINITIONS:

- **bit part** ... an opportunity for the actor with the smallest role to count everyone else's lines and mention repeatedly that he/she has the smallest part in the show.

- **blocking** ... moving actors around the stage so as not to collide with walls, furniture, orchestra pit or each other; similar to playing chess, except the pawns argue with the director.

- **criticophobia** ... a dread of critics.

- **dark spot** ... the stage area the lighting designer has unaccountably neglected to light but which has a magnetic attraction for the first-time actor; a dark spot is never evident before opening night.

- **eternity** ... the time that passes between a dropped cue and the next line.

- **monologue** ... that shining moment when all eyes are focused on a single actor desperately aware that if they forget a line, nothing can save them.

- **prop** ... a hand-carried object small enough to be lost by an actor fifteen seconds before it is needed onstage.

- **quality theater** ... any show with which you were directly involved.

- **theatrophobia** ... an aversion to theatres and plays.

- **turkey** ... every show with which you were not directly involved.

THE COMMON THEATRE expression for pay day is "What time does the ghost walk?" — a code phrase used among actors to establish the time of pay call. This has a practical reason, as actors were suspicious of outsiders knowing they might have money on their person or backstage. "Ghost" was also a term for the company treasurer and the "ghost window" was the window where actors received their pay.

USEFUL TECH TIP: Beware of lighting designers nicknamed "The Prince of Darkness".

"WHOEVER CONDEMNS the theatre is an enemy to his country."
 — *Voltaire*

"CURTAIN! Fast music! Light! Ready for the last finale! Great! The show looks good, the show looks good!"
 — *final words of Florenz Ziegfeld*

HEAR BROADWAY'S BIGGEST SHOW!

ZIEGFELD FOLLIES

OF THE AIR

Glorifying the American Girl!

FANNIE BRICE
Laugh with America's
most popular comedienne

BENNY FIELDS
Hear Broadway's newest
singing sensation!

AL GOODMAN'S ORCHESTRA—PATTI CHAPIN
and a chorus of famous *ZIEGFELD FOLLIES GIRLS*

WABC EVERY SATURDAY **8 TO 9 P. M., EST**
COLUMBIA NETWORK—COAST-TO-COAST
PRESENTED BY THE MAKERS OF PALMOLIVE SOAP

~ ACKNOWLEDGMENTS ~

Special thanks for information on traditions and superstitions to: Ken Costigan, Pamela Ross, Barry Kornhauser, Michael Greer, Nancy Hess, Tom and Barb Evans, Tami Swartz, Jane Ridley, Deb Cerruti.

Very special thanks to our parents and families, all the amazing theatre folk we've ever known (and still hope to meet) … and to our special friend and theatrical lodestar, Kathleen Bishop.

~ THE AUTHORS ~

Lisa Bansavage is an actress whose career comprises Broadway, Off Broadway, regional theatre, film, television and national commercial credits including *Master Class*, *A Man for All Seasons*, *The Grapes of Wrath*, *Grace & Glorie*, *Mastergate*, *Red Scare on Sunset*, *The Changeling*, *The Country Wife*, *A View from the Bridge*, *The Beauty Queen of Leenane*, *The Sisters Rosenweig*, *Night of the Iguana*, *A Time to Kill*, *Married to the Mob*, *Three Men and a Baby*, *The Fisher King*, *Diary of Anne Frank*, *Vampire Lesbians of Sodom*, *The Loman Family Picnic*, *Law and Order/Criminal Intent* and a third of the full Shakespearean canon as well as a role opposite Sir Anthony Quayle in the BBC-London production of *An Exchange of Gifts*.

She is a proud graduate of Carnegie-Mellon University's theatre conservatory and holds a Masters in Theatre from the University of Pittsburgh where she was the Merrill Fellow.

Today, she utilizes her theatrical skills and stage experience pursuing a successful career as an Interfaith minister and ceremonial officiant. **www.revbansavage.com**

L.E. McCullough, Ph.D. is an educator, playwright, composer and ethnomusicologist whose studies in music and folklore have spanned cultures throughout the world. Dr. McCullough is the former Administrative Director of the Humanities Theatre Group at Indiana University-Purdue University at Indianapolis and current Director of Pages of History in Woodbridge, New Jersey.

Since 1991 Dr. McCullough has received 48 awards in 32 national literary competitions and had 182 poem and short story publications in 92 North American literary journals. Winner of the 1995 Emerging Playwright Award for the New York premiere of his stage play *Blues for Miss Buttercup*, Dr. McCullough is the author of more than 176 plays on history, folklore and current events published in 31 books of original stage monologues, children's plays and stories by Smith & Kraus, EduPress and Regina Press including *Ice Babies in Oz; Plays of America for Young Actors; Plays of America for Children; Plays of the Songs of Christmas; Plays of the Wild West, Vols. 1 & 2; Plays from Fairy Tales; Plays from Mythology; Plays of People at Work; Plays of Exploration and Discovery; Stories of the Songs of Christmas; Anyone Can Produce Plays with Kids; "Now I Get It!", Curriculum Plays Vol. 1 & 2; 111 1-Minute Monologues for Teens; 111 1-Minute Monologues for Pre-Teens; Plays of Ancient Israel; Plays of Israel Reborn; Wild & Wacky Monologues for Kids.*

He is co-author with Claude McNeal of *American Cabaret and the New Theatre of Conscience* and co-editor with Lisa Bansavage and Jill Swanson of *111 Shakespeare Monologues for Teens* and *60 Great Shakespeare Scenes for Teens*.

Dr. McCullough's plays are performed in the U.S., Canada, Africa, Australia and Europe — in schools, churches, synagogues, community centers, festivals, museums, historical societies and theatre venues of all kind. For full publication and performance credits see **www.educationalclassroomplays.com**.